Pebble® Plus

Construction Zone

Building a Bridge

by JoAnn Early Macken

Consulting Editor: Gail Saunders-Smith, PhD

Consultant: Dr. Karen C. Chou, P.E.
Professor of Civil Engineering, Minnesota State University, Mankato
Structural Engineer, Paulsen Architects
Mankato, Minnesota

Capstone press®

Mankato, Minnesota

Pebble Plus is published by Capstone Press,
151 Good Counsel Drive, P.O. Box 669, Mankato, Minnesota 56002.
www.capstonepress.com

1 2 3 4 5 6 14 13 12 11 10 09

Library of Congress Cataloging-in-Publication Data
Macken, JoAnn Early, 1953–
    Building a bridge / by JoAnn Early Macken.
    p. cm. — (Pebble Plus. Construction zone)
    Includes bibliographical references and index.
    Summary: "Simple text and photographs present the construction of a bridge, including information on the
workers and equipment needed" — Provided by publisher.
    ISBN-13: 978-1-4296-2257-8 (hardcover)
    ISBN-10: 1-4296-2257-1 (hardcover)
    1. Bridges — Design and construction — Juvenile literature. I. Title.
TG148.M275 2009
624.2 — dc22   2008027656

Editorial Credits
Megan Peterson, editor; Ted Williams, designer; Jo Miller, photo researcher

Photo Credits
Alamy/Anthony Eva, 13; Dennis MacDonald, 19
BigStockPhoto.com/Icjtripod, 11
fotolia/Gilles Paire, 1; Karin Lau, cover, 15
Getty Images Inc./Iconica/Ghislain & Marie David de Lossy, 7; Stone/Bill Pogue, 17; Stone/James Martin, 5
Jupiterimages Corporation, 9
Shutterstock/iofoto, 21

Note to Parents and Teachers

The Construction Zone set supports national science standards related to science and
technology. This book describes and illustrates bridge construction. The images support early
readers in understanding the text. The repetition of words and phrases helps early readers learn
new words. This book also introduces early readers to subject-specific vocabulary words, which
are defined in the Glossary section. Early readers may need assistance to read some words and
to use the Table of Contents, Glossary, Read More, Internet Sites, and Index sections of
the book.

Table of Contents

Bridges

Cars, trucks, trains,
and people cross bridges.
New bridges are being built
all the time.

4

A city needs a new

suspension bridge.

Bridge engineers study

the land, wind, and traffic.

Then they design the bridge.

6

Working in Water

Tugboats bring

huge steel boxes

to the new bridge site.

These boxes, called caissons,

sink into the water.

9

Pumps inside the caissons
push out the water.
Cranes dig deep down
to solid rock.

crane

Foundations and Towers

Workers pour concrete
into the caissons.
Concrete gives the new bridge
strong foundations.

A tower crane lifts pieces
of steel and concrete.
The crane builds towers
on the foundations.

14

tower crane

15

Cables and Decks

Workers pull steel cables

across the towers.

They bury the ends

in concrete blocks

to keep the bridge steady.

tower

cables

17

Cranes lift the deck pieces.

Cables hold

the pieces in place.

The deck pieces become

the new road.

deck piece

The bridge is finished.

Now people can get

where they need to go.

Glossary

cable — a thick wire

caisson — a tube or box in which people and machines can work under water; caissons are later filled with concrete and used to support bridges and buildings.

concrete — a mixture of cement, water, sand, and gravel that hardens when it dries

crane — a machine with a long arm used to lift and move heavy objects

deck — a floor or platform; a bridge deck is the road vehicles travel on.

engineer — a person who uses science and math to plan, design, or build

foundation — a base on which something rests or is built

tower — a tall structure that holds up bridge cables

Read More

Nelson, Robin. *From Cement to Bridge.* Start to Finish. Minneapolis: Lerner, 2004.

Simon, Seymour. *Bridges.* Seemore Readers. San Francisco: SeaStar Books, 2005.

Tieck, Sarah. *Brooklyn Bridge.* All Aboard America. Edina, Minn.: Abdo, 2008.

Internet Sites

FactHound offers a safe, fun way to find educator-approved Internet sites related to this book.

Here's what you do:

1. Visit *www.facthound.com*
2. Choose your grade level.
3. Begin your search.

This book's ID number is 9781429622578.

FactHound will fetch the best sites for you!

Index

cables, 16, 18

caissons, 8, 10, 12

cars, 4

concrete, 12, 14, 16

cranes, 10, 14, 18

deck pieces, 18

engineers, 6

foundations, 12, 14

pumps, 10

steel, 8, 14, 16

towers, 14, 16

traffic, 6

trains, 4

trucks, 4

tugboats, 8

wind, 6

Word Count: 147
Grade: 1
Early-Intervention Level: 22

24